Meals in Minutes

100+ Recipes Featuring Thrive Life Freeze-Dried Foods

JODI WEISS
TRACY TAYLOR
CHRISTINA RIOSTIRADO

Copyright © 2019 Pantry Pack Club
Christina Riostirado, Tracy Taylor, Jodi Weiss

All rights reserved.

ISBN: 9781704638225

DEDICATIONS

To my four kids: Mikey, Lexi, James, and Izzy. They are my biggest cheerleaders, they taste test all of my recipes, and they help out when I'm busy working on projects like this one. This book would have never come together without them!

And a special thanks to my parents who taught me how to work hard, dream big, and never give up!

-Jodi

....

To my family and all the extras that come through my doors and gather to celebrate. You have given me the desire to feed and feast and that desire has made this project so much fun.

Special thanks to Jon, William, Jonathan and Andrew for being my daily taste testers and to my parents for always teaching me that the best things happen when you gather in the kitchen.

-Tracy

....

To my loves: Rick, Isabela and Rico. They make it easy to pursue my dreams and to work in a profession that I love. To my Parents who watch my kiddos when I'm out sharing Thrive, teaching people to use it and whenever I have a ton of work to do, they take them so I can concentrate and work! Without them and their support, I wouldn't be able to do what I love so much!

-Christina

Table of Contents

Introduction 1

About Thrive Life 3

Potluck Pack 7

Camping Prep Pack 19

Picnics, Pools, & Parties Pack 31

Around the World Pack 43

Back to School Pack 55

Blast from the Past Pack 93

Cinco de Mayo Pack 105

Bonus Recipes 113

Appendix: Equivalents & Substitutions 126

Index (by Recipe Type) 128

Introduction

Welcome to the Meals in Minutes Cookbook. We are so excited that you made the choice to pick up this particular book. This book is different from other recipe books ... but that is what makes it so wonderful!

All of the recipes in this book contain freeze-dried foods. Now if you think that is just for astronauts or for hikers ... think again! Cooking with freeze-dried foods can make you a wizard in the kitchen and can save your family's mealtime. With all of your fruits and veggies pre-washed and chopped, all your meats thawed and cooked, you will be able to put together gourmet meals ... IN MINUTES!

The brand of freeze-dried foods we use is Thrive Life. Chapter two will go into more details on why we choose this particular brand ... but the truth is, Thrive is what brought the three of us together and started the whole idea for this book.

Thrive Life is a direct sales company and the three of us all earned a trip to Panama last year. The three of us did not all work together prior to the trip, and were not even on the same team, but we hit it off and immediately started sharing ideas about our business and tricks for using this food to make fantastic recipes. We live in opposite ends of North America but we now talk daily and came up with the brilliant idea of creating ... The Pantry Pack Club!

The Pantry Pack Club is an exclusive community we created for our customers because we were having so much fun sharing ideas with each other that we wanted to spread it to even more people. Every month we pick a theme and create 10 printable recipes around that theme based on the monthly specials from Thrive Life. We encourage our members to post pictures of the recipes they are trying and we do fun giveaways just for being active participants in the group.

After six months of posting our "pantry packs" in our Facebook group we realized that our recipe binders were getting full and we had lots of people who were wanting to enjoy the recipes that weren't in the group. So we compiled everything into this book and opened it up to the public!

We are so excited to share our love of Thrive Life freeze-dried foods with you. Just because the food will last 25 years on your shelf, doesn't mean it should. Let's get cooking!

About Thrive Life

Now that you've gotten to know us a little bit, we want to go into a little more detail about why freeze dried foods are our favorite to cook with. By using these foods you can create healthy and quicker versions of your family's favorite meals ... or use the ones we create and try something new!

So how does Thrive Life stack up against the grocery store? We will let you in on a secret. Not only is there more color, more flavor, and more nutrients....

It's healthier. The vitamins and nutrients are locked in so your food stays fresher.

It's tastier. The produce is as ripe and flavorful as the day it was picked.

It's fresher. No mold or slime. Freeze dried food stay fresh even without preservatives.

It's easier. No more washing, peeling, shopping, thawing.... The list goes on. Say goodbye to prep time, we have more important things to do.

It's wastelessier. With a long shelf life, these foods will not go rotten in your fridge. No more letting your food (and $) go to waste.

What makes Thrive Life stand apart from other freeze-dried food companies? Their exclusive 40 step Nutrilock process makes all the difference.

Thrive has its own in-house freeze-drying machines, so they are able to source food from the best suppliers. Thrive partners with farmers who make quality food their passion. They harvest produce at its nutritional peak. It's then flash frozen within hours. No more picking things before they are ripe and allowing them to sit on a truck for weeks.

Once the food arrives at the state of the art Thrive Life facility the nutrients and flavor are locked in during the proprietary freeze drying process. All foods are tested for taste and quality as well as for bacteria and other contaminents mulitple times throughout the process, so you never have to worry about recalls and can be assured that your food is safe to eat.

Thrive Life's goal is to ensure the highest quality ingredients are available for you. OUR goal is to ensure you know how to use them. We created this book to help you create masterpieces in your own kitchen. We want to help you take the stress out of mealtime and we will show you exactly how to do that!

What's the best way to get Thrive Life foods in your home? Get started today with the DELIVERY SERVICE! Thrive's delivery service is an auto-ship program like no other you've heard of. You can pause, skip a shipment, or cancel at any time! Say what? But as long as your delivery account is active you are eligible for benefits such as exclusive sale items each month and FREE SHIPPING on orders over $100.

The biggest perk of being on the delivery service as one of our customers is you get to be a part of the Pantry Pack Club and get more recipes like the ones in this book every month FOR FREE. Plus it's a fun community where you can share what you are cooking and win prizes in our giveaways.

CHOOSE WHO TO SIGN UP WITH!

Christina Riostirado

https://thechillypantry.thrivelife.com/delivery/index/deliveryservice/

Tracy Taylor

https://tracytaylor.thrivelife.com/delivery/index/deliveryservice/

Jodi Weiss

https://jodiandjulie.thrivelife.com/delivery/index/deliveryservice/

ONCE YOU HAVE A DELIVERY JOIN THE CLUB:
https://www.facebook.com/groups/pantrypackclub/

"I love pantry pack club with Tracy, Christina, and Jodi! I live in a small town and getting fresh produce is difficult. With the freeze dried foods from Thrive, I can always have veggies and fruits on hand for when the produce at the stores are rotten already. P.S. The Chicken Salad To Go's are really really good!!"

~Elizabeth Nelner,
Pantry Pack Club Member

Potluck Pack

Apple Pie Smoothie
Apple Pinto Bean Tart
Blackberry Apple Crumble
Blackberry Cornmeal Muffins
Carrot Pineapple Muffins
Chicken & Bean Chili
Chicken Noodle Soup Meal-in-a-Jar
Curried Cauliflower
Homemade Cornbread
Loaded Cauliflower

Apple Pie Smoothie

Serves 1

2 cups Thrive Fuji Apples
1/2 cup Quick Oats
1 cup Milk (Almond or Regular)
1 cup Ice
1 tsp Ground Cinnamon
Pinch of Nutmeg
Pinch of Ground Ginger
**Optional 1-2 tsp Honey (or Sweetener of Choice)

Powder apples and oats in a blender. Add all other ingredients and blend until smooth.

Apple Pinto Bean Tart

Serves 6

1 1/2 cups Thrive Fuji Apples (+5 Slices)
1/2 cup Brown Sugar
1 tbsp Lemon Juice
1/4 tsp Ground Nutmeg
1/4 tsp Cinnamon
1/2 tsp Salt
2 tbsp Thrive Scrambled Egg Mix
1 1/2 cups Cooked Pinto Beans (about 3/4 Cups dry)
2 tbsp Maple Syrup
1 cup Water

Pre-heat oven to 350. Grease glass pie plate and set aside. In small bowl refresh the five slices of Fuji Apple for garnish. Set aside. Powder the 1 ½ cups of apples leaving small chunks. Mash up beans until they form a creamy paste. Add all the rest of the ingredients. Mix well.

Pour into prepared pie plate. Add refreshed apples to the top and sprinkle with sugar to crystallize. Bake for 30 minutes. Allow to cool and become firm before cutting. Serve with ice cream or whipped cream.

Blackberry Apple Crumble

Serves 1

1/2 cup Thrive Blackberries
1/2 cup Thrive Fuji Apples, broken into pieces
1 tsp Thrive Honey Crystals
1/2 cup Boiling Water (to refresh)

Crumble:
1/2 cup Quick Oats
1 tbsp Butter
1 tbsp Flour
1 tsp Brown Sugar

Pre-heat oven to 350 degrees. Combine crumble ingredients in a small bowl and set aside.

In a small baking dish combine fruit, honey crystals, and boiling water. Wait a few minutes until fruit is refreshed.

Sprinkle with the crumble and bake for 20 minutes.

Blackberry Cornmeal Muffins

Makes 12 Muffins

2 cups Flour (can use half white half whole wheat)
1 cup Thrive Cornmeal
1/2 cup Brown Sugar, firmly packed
1 tbsp Baking Powder
1 tbsp Baking Soda
3/4 tsp Salt
1 1/2 cups Plain Yogurt (Low-Fat if desired)
1/3 cup Vegetable Oil
3 tbsp Thrive Honey Crystals
2 tsp Vanilla
3 Eggs
2 heaping cups Thrive Blackberries

Preheat oven to 375 degrees. Grease 12 muffins cups.

Whisk together first 7 ingredients in large bowl. Combine yogurt, oil, honey crystals, vanilla, and eggs in a separate bowl. Add wet ingredients to dry and mix with spoon or spatula until combined. Fold in blackberries (crush slightly if you like smaller pieces).

Fill muffin cups to the top and bake for 10 minutes. Rotate pans and bake 10-12 minutes longer until slightly golden.

Cool for 5 minutes before transferring to cooling rack.

Carrot Pineapple Muffins

Makes 12 Muffins

2 cups All-Purpose Flour
1 1/4 cup White Sugar
2 tsp Baking Soda
2 tsp Ground Cinnamon
1/4 tsp Salt
2 cups Thrive Carrots, refreshed
1 cup Thrive Pineapple, broken smaller and refreshed
1/2 cup Raisins (optional)
3 Eggs
1 cup Vegetable Oil
2 tsp Vanilla

Pre-heat oven to 350. Grease 12 muffin cups.

In a large bowl, mix together flour, sugar, baking soda, cinnamon, and salt. Stir in refreshed pineapple, carrots and raisins (if desired).

In a separate bowl, beat eggs, oil, and vanilla. Stir egg mixture into the carrot/flour mixture just until moistened.

Scoop into prepared muffin cups and bake for 20 minutes or until toothpick inserted comes out clean.

Chicken & Bean Chili

Serves 4

1 cup Thrive Pinto Beans
1 tsp Salt
1 cup Thrive Chopped Onions, divided
4 tsp Minced Garlic, divided
2 cups Thrive Seasoned Chicken Slices
1/4 cup Thrive Green Chili Peppers
1 cup Salsa Verde
1/4 cup Thrive Cilantro
3 tbsp Thrive Chicken Bouillon
1 tsp Thrive Chef's Choice Seasoning
1 cup Thrive Sweet Corn
6 cups Water

Soak 1 cup of beans overnight. Drain and cover with fresh water. Add salt, 1/2 cup onion and 2 tsp garlic. Cook for 2 hours or until beans are tender. Drain when finished cooking.

Sauté chicken, 1/2 cup onion and 2 tsp garlic in a large pot or Dutch Oven (no need to refresh first). Add green chili peppers, Salsa Verde, cilantro, bouillon, Chef's Choice, corn, and water.

Add beans to the chicken mixture and bring to a boil. Simmer on low for 20 minutes.

Chicken Noodle Soup Meal-in-a-Jar

Serves 4-5

2 tbsp Thrive Chicken Bouillon
2 tsp Thrive Chef's Choice Seasoning
2 tsp Thrive Salad Seasoning Blend
1 tsp Salt (or more to taste)
1/4 cup Thrive Chopped Onions
1/4 cup Thrive Carrots (optional)
1/2 cup Thrive Celery
1 cup Thrive Chopped Chicken
2 cup Thrive Egg Noodle Pasta

To Make Jar: Add ingredients to jar in order listed for a pretty jar, add in reverse order if you'd like to pack in a few more noodles to bulk it up.

To Prepare: Bring 8 cups of water to a boil in a large saucepan. Add jar ingredients and simmer for 10-12 minutes (may need longer if you use carrots).

Curried Cauliflower

Serves 2

1 cup Thrive Cauliflower
2 tbsp Coconut Oil, melted
1 tbsp Curry Powder
1 tbsp Ground Turmeric
1 tsp Salt
1/2 tsp Cayenne Pepper
Thrive Cilantro

Pre-heat oven to 350. In a large bowl, whisk together oil and spices (except cilantro). Add cauliflower and mix until coated.

Spread cauliflower in single layer on baking sheet. Bake for 15-20 until golden. Top with cilantro for garnish.

Homemade Cornbread

Makes 9 Slices

1/2 cup Butter, melted
2/3 cup Sugar
2 Eggs
1 cup Buttermilk
1/2 tsp Baking Soda
1 cup Thrive Cornmeal
1 cup All-Purpose Flour
1/2 tsp Salt

Preheat oven to 375. Grease a 9 x 9 square pan.

In a large bowl combine melted butter and white sugar. Quickly add eggs and beat until well blended. Combine buttermilk with baking soda and stir into egg mixture. Add cornmeal, flour, and salt and stir until well blended and only a few lumps remain.

Pour batter into the prepared pan. Bake for 25 to 30 minutes, or until a toothpick inserted in the center comes out clean.

Loaded Cauliflower

Serves 2

2 cups Thrive Cauliflower
1 tbsp Thrive Green Onions
1/2 cup Thrive Shredded Cheese
4 oz Cream Cheese, chunked
2 tbsp Bacon Crumbles

Pre-heat oven to 350.

Refresh cauliflower, green onions, and cheese. Add cream cheese and bacon crumbles. Stir lightly. Bake in a small casserole dish for 15 minutes or until cheese melts and can be mixed together.

"I love the pantry meals using freeze dried foods. Not only is it fast to put together a nutritious meal, there is absolutely no waste! I make them ahead at home and use them in our camper."

~Constance Beck,
Pantry Pack Club Member

Camping Prep Pack

Berries & Beans
Camping Quesadillas Meal-in-a-Jar
Egg Boats
Grilled Beans & Apple Salad
Mozzarella Green Bean Salad
Omelette-in-a-Bag
Peanut Butter & Jelly Smoothie
Sausage Noodle Salad-in-a-Jar
Tomato Broccoli Casserole
Tomato Soup & Cheesy Dippers

Berries & Beans

Serves 2

1 cup Thrive Green Beans, refreshed
1/2 cup Thrive Raspberries, refreshed
1 tbsp Orchard Apple (optional)
1 tbsp Butter
1/4 cup Chopped Walnuts or Shaved Almonds
1 tbsp Olive Oil
1/4 tsp Chopped Garlic
Salt and Pepper, to taste
1/4 cup Feta Cheese

In a medium bowl refresh green beans with 1/3 cup of water. In separate bowl refresh raspberries with 2 tbsp of water (you can sweeten with orchard apple or sweetener of choice). Drain any excess water once refreshed.

In a pan, heat butter, add chopped nuts and cook 2 minutes stirring often. Add olive oil and garlic. Toast until lightly brown.

Add refreshed green beans with salt and pepper to taste. Toss over heat for approximately 2 minutes. Remove from heat, mix in refreshed raspberries.

Sprinkle with feta cheese and serve!

Camping Quesadillas Meal-in-a-Jar

Serves 4-5

1 cup Thrive Chopped Chicken
1 1/2 cups Thrive Cheddar Cheese
2 tbsp Thrive Green Chili Peppers
1/4 cup Thrive Tomatoes
2 tbsp Thrive Chopped Onions
1 tsp Ground Cumin
1 tsp Chili Powder

3/4-1 cup Water
4-6 Medium Tortillas
1-2 cups Salsa
Sour Cream

To Make Jar: Prepare in a large jar or recycled Thrive Life pantry can. Scoop each of the first five ingredients into layers in jar. Put the spices in a small baggie and tuck into the top.

To Prepare: Remove spice baggie. Add 3/4-1 cup of hot water to jar. Stir or shake up to refresh. Add spices and stir well. Lay out tortillas on a piece of tin foil. Spread salsa and sour cream on tortilla. Add chicken mixture and fold over. Wrap in foil and put in campfire. Cook until cheese is melted. Enjoy!

Egg Boats

Serves 4

4 Buns or Roll of choice (Hotdog, Hamburger Buns, etc)
1/2 cup Thrive Scrambled Egg Mix
1 cup Water
1/4 cup Thrive Sausage Crumbles
1/2 cup Thrive Mozzarella Cheese
1/2 cup Omelette Fixings (Onions, Peppers, etc.)
Salt and Pepper, to taste

Preheat oven to 350 degrees.

In a medium sized bowl whisk scrambled egg mix with water. Add sausage, cheese and your favorite omelette fixings. If you are using Thrive veggies as fixings let them sit in egg to refresh.

While your fixings are refreshing, cut holes in your buns or baguette and remove the top. Press doughy part in to create a boat. **Be sure not to cut the bottom of the bun or mixture will leak out!

Fill buns with egg mixture. Bake for 25-28 minutes until set in the middle. Cool for 10 minutes, cut and serve.

Grilled Beans & Apple Salad

Serves 2

1 cup Thrive Green Beans
1 cup Thrive Fuji Apples
1 tbsp Olive Oil
1/2 cup Sliced Almonds
1 tbsp Orchard Apple (or sweetener or choice)
Maple Syrup (as topping)

In a bowl, refresh green beans and apples with 1 cup of water (add in Orchard Apple if you would like). Drain excess water once refreshed. Heat up olive oil in pan. Once hot, add bean and apple mixture along with almonds. Toss in pan to grill until starting to brown. Drizzle with maple syrup. Mix well and remove from heat. Enjoy!

Mozzarella Green Bean Salad

Serves 2

1 cup Thrive Green Beans, refreshed
1/2 cup Thrive Tomato Dices, refreshed
1/2 cup Mozzarella Cheese, refreshed
1 tbsp Basil
1-2 tbsp Italian Dressing

In a medium bowl, refresh beans with about 1/3 cup of HOT water to make them more tender. In a separate bowl refresh tomatoes, cheese and basil with 1/3 cup of COLD water. Allow to sit to refresh. Drain any remaining liquid from both bowls. combine beans, tomatoes, and cheese and toss with Italian dressing. Chill.

Omelette-in-a-Bag

Serves 1

6 tbsp Thrive Scrambled Egg Mix
3/4 cup Water
1 tbsp Thrive Sausage Crumbles
2 tbsp Thrive Broccoli
2 tbsp Thrive Mozzarella Cheese
Salt and Pepper, to taste
Medium Ziploc Freezer Bag

In a medium bowl whisk scrambled egg mix with water. Add broccoli, sausage, and cheese. Let sit while you boil 4 cups of water in saucepan (use a big enough pan so bag does not touch the sides).

Pour mixture into Ziploc bag, remove air and seal. Place in boiling water for 10-12 minutes. Remove when eggs are firm. Open bag, omelette should pour right out of bag when ready.

*You can use any combination of veggies, meats and cheeses for your omelette!

Peanut Butter & Jelly Smoothie

Serves 1

3 tbsp Thrive Peanut Flour
1 cup Almond or Regular Milk
2 tbsp Thrive Apple Orchard (or alternative sweetener)
1 cup Thrive Banana Slices
1/2 cup Thrive Raspberries
1 cup Ice

Mix all ingredients together and blend until smooth. Enjoy!

**After blended, put in seal-able pouch and freeze for an ice pack you can eat!

Sausage Noodle Salad Meal-in-a-Jar

Serves 2

3/4 cup Elbow Macaroni
3/4 cup Thrive Sausage Crumbles
1/2 cup Thrive Diced Tomatoes
1/2 cup Thrive Broccoli
2 tbsp Thrive Green Chili Peppers
1/2 tsp Garlic
1 pkg Mayonnaise
Salt and Pepper, to taste

To Make Jar: Use a pint-size mason jar. Layer the ingredients in the order listed. Add one packet of mayo to complete the jar. Seal well and label.

To Prepare: Dump contents of jar in saucepan and add 1 1/2 jars of water Bring to boil. Boil for 5 minutes. Reduce heat and simmer for 5 minutes. Cool and add mayo for cold or stir in mayo and enjoy warm!

Tomato Broccoli Casserole

Serves 4

2 cups Elbow Macaroni
1/2 tsp Minced Garlic
1/4 cup Thrive Chopped Onions
1 cup Thrive Broccoli
1 cup Thrive Tomatoes
2 cups Thrive Seasoned Chicken Slices
1/4 cup Thrive Basil
1/2 cup Thrive Mozzarella Cheese
Salt and Pepper to taste

Boil macaroni in 5 cups salted water with onions, garlic and chicken. When noodles are almost done add vegetables. Drain excess water. Add basil, pepper and salt. Cover with refreshed mozzarella. Put under broiler until cheese is melted.

Tomato Soup & Cheesy Dippers

Serves 2

Tomato Soup:
1 cup Thrive Diced Tomatoes
1 tsp Thrive Chopped Onions, powdered
1 cup Water
1/2 cup Heavy Cream
1/2 tsp Garlic Powder
1/2 tsp Thrive Basil
Salt and Pepper, to taste

In a medium saucepan combine all ingredients, bring to a boil. Then reduce heat and simmer for 10 minutes.

Cheesy Dippers:
Leftover buns or bread
1 cup Thrive Mozzarella Cheese, refreshed
Butter
Garlic Powder

Refresh mozzarella cheese with 1/2 cup of water. Let sit until refreshed. Cut up buns to desired size for dipping. Mix garlic powder with butter and spread over bread. Cover with cheese. Toast bread under broiler until cheese is melted and golden. To cook on an open fire, place bread in foil and cook until toasted. Dip in soup and enjoy!

"Cooking with Thrive has become a family affair in my household. As a busy single mom of four it's sometimes hard to get dinner on the table. Cooking with freeze-dried foods has allowed me to come up with so many Meals in Minutes that I can make on busy days or have my big kids cook!"

~Jodi Weiss,
Meals in Minutes Co-Author

Picnics, Pools & Parties Pack

Apple Cinnamon Muffins
Apricot Chicken
Apricot Jam/Topping/Compote
Buffalo Chicken Wraps
Chicken Bacon Ranch Salad
Chicken Parmigiana
Chicken Salad
Patriotic Jell-O
Red, White, & Blue Smoothie
Rice Pudding

Apple Cinnamon Muffins

Makes 12 Muffins

2 cups Thrive Granny Smith Apples, refreshed
2 tsp Baking Powder
1/2 cup Brown Sugar, packed
3 tsp Ground Cinnamon
1 1/8 cup Flour
1/2 tsp Salt
3/4 cup Sugar
1/2 cup Whole Wheat Flour
1 Egg
1/3 cup Vegetable or Canola Oil
1/3 cup Milk

Topping (optional):
1/4 cup Sugar
2 tbsp Flour
2 tbsp Butter (room temperature)
1 tsp Ground Cinnamon

Preheat oven to 400. Grease 12 muffin cups. Mix dry ingredients together. Add oil, milk and egg, and stir until combined. Fold in refreshed apples. Pour into muffin tins.

In small bowl, mix topping ingredients with fork and sprinkle over unbaked muffins. Bake 15-20 minutes. Enjoy!

Apricot Chicken

Serves 4

1 cup Thrive Seasoned Chicken Slices, refreshed
1/2 cup French or Catalina Salad Dressing
1/2 cup Apricot Jam (see our recipe!)
2 tbsp Dry Onion Soup Mix

In medium bowl mix dressing, jam, and onion soup mix together. Refresh chicken in 1/2 cup of hot water. Drain any excess liquid.

Add chicken and dressing mixture to medium sauce pan. Heat to simmer over medium heat for about 10 minutes, stirring occasionally. Serve over rice. Enjoy!

Apricot Jam / Topping / Compote

1 cup Thrive Apricots
1 cup Hot Water
1/4 cup + 2 tbsp Sugar (divided)
2 tbsp Pectin

In a mixing bowl, combine apricots, water, and 2 tbsp of sugar. Let sit for 30 minutes. Crush apricots with slotted spoon or potato masher.

In separate bowl, mix remaining 1/4 cup of sugar and pectin. Add in apricots and mix for 3 minutes.

Ladle into clean container or jar. Let sit for 30 minutes. Refrigerate or put in freezer to last longer.

Perfect to eat over ice cream, on toast or in our Apricot Chicken recipe.

Buffalo Chicken Wraps

Makes 2 Wraps

1 cup Thrive Seasoned Chicken Slices, refreshed
1/4 cup Buffalo Sauce
2 tbsp Ranch or Blue Cheese Dressing
Lettuce
2 Flour Tortillas

In medium bowl, refresh chicken with 1/2 cup hot water. Let sit for 5-8 minutes then drain any remaining liquid.

Mix in buffalo sauce and coat chicken well. Spoon into tortillas. Add chopped lettuce and drizzle with dressing of choice.

Additional wrap ideas:
*Add a little kick by adding 1 tbsp Thrive Green Chilies.
*Use blue cheese and add in 1 tbsp Thrive Celery.
*Add cheese!

Chicken Bacon Ranch Salad

Serves 4

2 cups Pasta, cooked al dente and drained
2 cups Thrive Seasoned Chicken Slices, refreshed
1 cup Thrive Green Peas, refreshed
1 cup Diced Tomatoes
6 slices Bacon, cooked and diced
1/2 cup Ranch Dressing
2 tbsp Mayonnaise
2 tbsp Sour Cream
1 tsp Pepper
1/4 tsp Salt

Cook pasta and drain. Refresh chicken and peas in about a cup and a half of water. Cook bacon, drain and dice. Add pasta, tomatoes, and bacon to bowl with chicken and peas. Mix well.

Stir in mayonnaise, sour cream, salt and pepper and mix well. Chill and serve!

Chicken Parmigiana

Serves 2

1 cup Thrive Seasoned Chicken Slices
1/2 cup Italian Bread Crumbs
Olive Oil

1 cup Hot Water
1/4 cup Thrive Tomato Sauce

2 cups Noodles, cooked and drained
1/2 cup Thrive Parmesan Cheese, refreshed
Italian Seasoning

Refresh chicken slices in 1/2 cup of hot water for about 10 minutes. Roll in bread crumbs. Pan fry in olive oil turning until brown.

In a small pan, bring water to boil and stir in tomato sauce until hot.

In baking dish, layer noodles, chicken, sauce and top with Parmesan cheese. Sprinkle with Italian seasoning and slide under broiler until cheese is melted. Enjoy!

Chicken Salad

Serves 2

1 cup Thrive Seasoned Chicken, broken into smaller pieces
3/4-1 tsp Thrive Chef's Choice Seasoning
1/4 cup Thrive Celery, broken into smaller pieces
3 tbsp Thrive Chopped Onions
3 tbsp Mayonnaise

In medium bowl, refresh chicken, celery, and onions in 3/4 cup of hot water. Let sit for 5-8 minutes. Mix in mayo and Chef's Choice. Mix well. Refrigerate or enjoy immediately.

Additional chicken salad ideas:
Add refreshed Thrive Grapes or Thrive Cranberries.
Add Thrive Green Chili Peppers for a kick.

Patriotic Jello

Makes a 9x13 Pan

2 3-oz pkg Blue Jello
1 1/2 cups Thrive Blueberries
2 envelopes Unflavored Gelatin (Knox brand)
14-oz can Eagle Sweetened Condensed Milk
2 3-oz pkg Strawberry Jello
1 1/2 cups Thrive Strawberry Slices
1 container Whipped Topping

Make your blue layer of jello. Mix 2 packages of blue jello with 2 cups of boiling water until dissolved. Then add 1 cup of ice cold water and stir. Pour into a 9×12 pan. Sprinkle blueberries evenly into the pan and stir them in so they are covered with liquid. Let set in fridge for 4 hours or overnight.

Make your white layer of jello. Sprinkle 2 envelopes of unflavored gelatin into 1/2 a cup of cold water. After it thickens, add 1 1/2 cups of boiling water and mix in until it dissolves. Stir in condensed milk until smooth. Let cool. Pour over hardened blue layer. Let chill for 4 hours or overnight.

Make your red layer of jello. Mix 2 packages of red jello with 2 cups of boiling water until dissolved. Then add 1 cup of ice cold water and stir. Sprinkle strawberries into the liquid. Pour entire mixture over top of white layer. Let set in fridge for 4 hours or overnight.

Once the red layer has set firmly, spread whipped topping like frosting, then create flag with refreshed strawberries/blueberries.

Red, White, & Blue Smoothie

Serves 1

1/2 cup Thrive Blueberries, refreshed
3 tbsp Water
1/3 cup Ice
Blend & layer in glass.

3/4 cup Vanilla Yogurt
Blend and layer in glass.

3/4 cup Thrive Strawberry Slices, refreshed
1/2 cup Water
1/2 cup Ice
Blend and layer in glass.

Lazy Cook Version: Put fruit and yogurt in blender, add 1 cup of water, 1 cup of ice and blend! Not as pretty but still as yummy!!!

Rice Pudding

Serves 3-4

2 Eggs, beaten
1/2 cup Sugar
1/4 tsp Salt
2 cups Milk
1 1/4 cups Thrive Rice, cooked and cooled
1/2 cup Raisins (optional)
Cinnamon and Nutmeg, to taste

Preheat oven to 325 degrees. Mix all the ingredients together and pour into a greased 1 qt. bowl. Set the bowl in a shallow pan. Pour hot water into the pan about 1 inch deep.

Put pan into the oven and bake for 1 ½ hours.

Optional: Use Apricot Compote as a topping!

"I love the Pantry Pack club because it has taught me how to use the food storage and now I know if I don't have something for a recipe in the fridge or pantry I just go to my food storage and usually what I need is there. I love the recipes. So many great ideas I would have never thought of and so tasty and husband approved."

~Marilyn Myers,
Pantry Pack Club Member

Around the World Pack

Cornbread Applesauce Muffins
Dutch Apple Baby
Ground Beef & Potato Casserole
Ground Beef Stroganoff
Jamaican Beef Patties
Pork Goulash Meal-in-a-Jar
Pulled Pork Sliders
Sweet and Sour Pulled Pork
Taco-in-a-Bag
Tourtière

Cornbread Applesauce Muffins

(Native American-Inspired)

Makes 6 Muffins

1/2 cup Thrive Cornmeal
1/2 cup Whole Wheat Flour
1/2 tsp Baking Soda
1/2 tsp Salt
6 tbsp Thrive Applesauce
1/2 cup Water
1/2 cup Milk or Almond Milk
2 tbsp Maple Syrup

Pre-heat oven to 350 degrees. Fill muffin pan with liners or spray with cooking spray.

Combine all ingredients in a bowl. Mix until combined. Fill muffin cups 3/4 full and bake for 25-28 minutes or until toothpick comes out clean. Immediately transfer muffins from pan to cooling rack.

Enjoy!

Dutch Apple Baby

Makes 2 Pies

2/3 cup Thrive Applesauce
1/2 cup Thrive Scrambled Egg Mix
3 tbsp Thrive Instant Milk
1 cup Flour
1/2 tsp Salt
1/4 cup Sugar
1/4 cup Thrive Butter Powder (or Melted Butter)
4 cups Water

Pre-Heat oven to 400 degrees.

Mix all ingredients together and pour into two 9-inch greased glass pie plates. Bake for 20 minutes and serve with toppings of your choice.

Try with a scoop of applesauce and whipping cream with cinnamon. Enjoy!

Ground Beef & Potato Casserole

(English)

Serves 3-4

1 1/2 cup Thrive Potato Dices, refreshed
1 1/2 cup Thrive Ground Beef, refreshed
1 1/2 cup Thrive Cheddar Cheese, refreshed
1 can Cream of Chicken Soup
1-2 tbsp Sour Cream
1 tbsp Thrive Chopped Onions
1 tsp Chopped Garlic
Pinch of Thrive Chef's Choice Seasoning

Pre-heat oven to 350 degrees. Grease a 9x9 dish.

Refresh potatoes with 3/4 cup cold water. Refresh ground beef with 3/4 cup warm water. Refresh cheddar cheese with 3/4 cup cold water. Once refreshed, drain any remaining liquid off of potatoes, beef, and cheese. Whisk soup, sour cream, onions, and spices.

Layer the ingredients as follows: 1/3 of potatoes, 1/3 of meat, 1/3 third of soup mix and 1/3 cheese. Repeat twice.

Cover with foil sprayed with non stick spray on casserole side. Place on baking sheet and cook for 30 minutes. Uncover and return to oven for five more minutes.

* Add an extra handful of cheese for the last five minutes.
* Add bacon and green onions for a full baked potato experience!

Ground Beef Stroganoff

(Russian-Inspired)

Serves 4-5

1/3 cup Thrive Bechamel Sauce
2 tbsp Thrive Espagnole Gravy
1/3 cup Thrive Sour Cream Powder
2 tbsp Thrive Beef Bouillon
2 tsp Dill Weed
3/4 cup Thrive Ground Beef
2 cups Thrive Egg Noodle Pasta
1/3 cup Thrive Mushrooms (optional)

In a large saucepan bring 5 ½ cups of water to a boil. Add all ingredients and let simmer for 15-20 minutes. Let stand for 5 minutes to thicken.

Jamaican Beef Patties

Serves 2

1 cup Thrive Ground Beef
1 tbsp Red/Green Bell Peppers
1/2 tbsp Thrive Chopped Onions
1/2 tbsp Thrive Green Onions
2 tbsp Lard or Bacon Fat
1 tbsp Curry Powder
1 tbsp Soy Sauce
1 tbsp Thrive Scrambled Egg Mix
3/4 cup Warm Water
Phyllo Pastry Dough (refrigerated)

Pre-heat oven to 400 degrees. Refresh all Thrive ingredients except scrambled eggs in 1/2 cup of water.

In large frying pan melt lard or bacon fat. Add refreshed Thrive ingredients, sauté until meat is browned. Drain the fat. Add soy sauce, curry, eggs, and water. Cook until heated through. Let cool.

Flatten out the pastry and cut into sections big enough for patties. Place filling in the middle of the pastry, pull over and seal the edges with a fork using a small amount of egg wash. (Make egg wash by mixing an additional 1 tsp of scrambled egg mix with a little bit of water).

Place all the patties on a cookie sheet and brush more egg wash over top of them. Bake for 20 minutes. Enjoy!

Pork Goulash Meal-in-a-Jar

(Hungarian-Inspired)

Serves 1

1/4 cup Thrive Pulled Pork
1/4 cup Thrive Sweet Corn
1/4 cup Thrive Tomato Powder
1 tsp Thrive Chopped Onions
1/4 tsp Thrive Italian Seasoning
1/4 tsp Garlic Powder
Dash Salt and Pepper
1/2 cup Thrive Egg Noodles, cooked
Sprinkle of Parmesan Cheese (optional)

To Make Jar: Place all ingredients except egg noodles and water in a 1/2 pint mason jar.

To Prepare: Cook egg noodles. While the noodles are cooking bring 1 1/2 cups water to boil in a small sauce pan. Dump in contents of jar. Heat for 3-5 minutes.

Stir in cooked egg noodles and mix. Sprinkle with Parmesan cheese and enjoy!

Tips: Try adding some red bell peppers and Hungarian Paprika to give it a more authentic Hungarian flavor!

To kettle cook right IN the jar, use a pint sized jar and include noodles. Add boiling water, stir, and put the top back on. Let sit 15 minutes to "cook" noodles. Great for on the go!

Pulled Pork Sliders

(American)

Makes 4 Sliders

1 cup Thrive Pulled Pork
1/2 cup Thrive Applesauce
1 tbsp Thrive Chopped Onions
1/2 cup BBQ Sauce
2 cups Water

Put ingredients in slow cooker for 30 minutes. Serve on a slider bun with coleslaw.

Enjoy!

Sweet and Sour Pulled Pork

(Asian-Inspired)

Serves 2

1 cup Thrive Pulled Pork, refreshed
2 tbsp Olive Oil
1 tbsp Minced Garlic
3 cups Water
1/2 cup Thrive Carrots
1/2 cup Thrive Red Bell Peppers
1/2 cup Thrive Onion Slices
1/2 cup Thrive Pineapple
1 tbsp Thrive Green Chili Peppers

Sauce:
1/2 cup Ketchup
2 tbsp Rice Vinegar
1 cup Pineapple Juice
2 tbsp Soy Sauce
2 tbsp Corn Starch
1/4 cup Cold Water

Refresh pork with 1/2 cup of hot water, set aside. In large sauce pan add olive oil and garlic. Heat. Add 3 cups of water, bring to a boil. Add all Thrive vegetables and refreshed pork. Simmer.

In a separate bowl combine ketchup, vinegar, pineapple juice, and soy sauce. Add to simmering mixture, bring back to a boil. In a small bowl whisk corn starch into cold water. Add to boiling mixture stirring to thicken. Remove from heat, let rest for 5 minutes. Serve over rice and eat with chopsticks. Enjoy!

Taco-in-a-Bag

(Mexican-Inspired)

Makes 3-4 Tacos

1 cup Thrive Ground Beef
1 tbsp Thrive Green Chili Peppers
1 tbsp Thrive Chopped Onions
1 tbsp Taco Seasoning
1 cup Water
3-4 Single Serving Doritos Bags

In medium skillet, add all ingredients with water. Heat on medium heat until completely refreshed and warm.

Break up Doritos in the bag, add meat mixture, cheese, salsa and lettuce.

Enjoy!

Tourtière

(French-Canadian-Inspired)

Makes 1 Pie

1 1/2 cups Thrive Ground Beef
1 cup Thrive Potato Dices
1/2 cup Thrive Carrots
1 tbsp Thrive Chopped Onions
1/4 cup Thrive Scrambled Egg Mix
1/4 tsp Cinnamon
1/4 tsp Nutmeg
1/4 tsp Ground Cloves
1 tsp Salt
1/2 tsp Dry Mustard
1/2 cup Butter, cubed (optional)
1/2 cup Vegetable Shortening, cubed (optional)
2 Pre-Made Pie Crusts

Preheat oven to 350 degrees. Grease a deep, glass pie plate and place one pie shell in the bottom.

In a medium-sized bowl, refresh beef, potato dices, carrots, onions, and scrambled egg mix in about 2 cups of water. Let sit for ten minutes. Add butter/shortening and spices. Mix well.

Make an egg wash by mixing an additional teaspoon of scrambled egg mix with water in a small bowl.

Fill pie shell with the mixture and use egg wash to seal second shell on top. Wash the top of pie shell with egg wash and add slits for venting. Bake 30 minutes. Enjoy.

"Thrive has become such a positive part of our lives, It allows me to provide the healthiest of foods to my family in a quick and easy manner which allows us to have more quality time together. We spend a lot of time outdoors and at camp, so shelf stable meals and snacks cut down on the amount we have to pack each week. Thrive also allows us to pack enough with us when we travel to ensure that we can both eat well and reduce costs of eating out every meal

We also have a great time creating new recipes and altering family favourites to incorporate Thrive Life. This book is partially a result of that passion."

~Tracy Taylor,
Meals in Minutes Co-Author

Back to School Pack

Apple Pear Cobbler
Beef Fajitas Meal-in-a-Jar
Beef Philly Cheesesteak Meal-in-a-Jar
Blackberry Mini Pies
Broccoli & Cheese Rice in-a-Mug
Buffalo Ranch Chicken w/ Blue Cheese Flatbread
Chicken & Green Mushroom Soup
Chicken Fajita Scramble
Chicken Mushroom Gravy
Chocolate Banana Mini Loaves
Cornbread Casserole
Creamy Nutrapacked Oats
Crock Pot Chicken Pot Pie
Easy Beef & Broccoli
Easy Taco Pasta
Food Truck Pulled Pork Over Mac & Cheese
Frozen Breakfast Pops
Hamburger Helper Meal-in-a-Jar
Hawaiian Pizza
Home-Flavored Yogurt
Loaded Potato Soup-in-a-Mug
Mexican Breakfast Bowl
Mrs. McG's Breakfast Sandwiches
Mrs. McG's Fruity Macaroons
Mrs. McG's Stuffed Peppers
Peach Coffee Cake
Peanut Butter Energy Balls
Pesto-Mato-Tato Chicken
Rice & Black Bean Bake Dinner
Sausage Quinoa Stir Fry
Sausage Pineapple Casserole
Scalloped Potatoes-in-a-Ja
Strawberry Oatmeal Bars
Street Corn Salad
Vegetable Beef Soup
Zucchini Corn Medley

Apple Pear Cobbler

By Kelly H.

Serves 1

2 tbsp Granola
2 tbsp Thrive Quick Oats
2 tbsp Thrive Fuji Apples
1 tbsp Thrive Granny Smith Apples
2 tbsp Brown Sugar
1 tbsp Thrive Pears
1/2 tsp Cinnamon
1 tbsp Thrive Vanilla Yogurt Bites

Stir together and enjoy! You can eat dry as a snack or add a bit of water and enjoy it as a meal.

Beef Fajitas Meal-in-a-Jar

By Cathy I.

Serves 4

2 cups Thrive Beef Slices
1 cup Thrive Green Bell Peppers
1 cup Thrive Red Bell Peppers
1/4 cup Thrive Chopped Onions
1/2 pkg 14 oz Fajita Seasoning

2 tbsp Oil
2 2/3 cups Hot Water
Soft Taco Shells

To Make Jar: Layer first 5 ingredients in a jar and seal with foodsave jar lid attachment.

To Prepare: In a skillet, add oil and heat it up. Dump contents of jar into pan and sauté for a few minutes. Add 2 2/3 Cups of hot water. Bring to slight boil, then simmer on low for about 15 minutes or until beef is completely refreshed.

Top with your favorite fajita toppings!

Beef Philly Cheesesteak Meal-in-a-Jar

Serves 4-5

1 cup Thrive Shredded Beef
1 cup Thrive Mozzarella Cheese
1/3 cup Thrive Green Bell Peppers
1/3 cup Thrive Mushroom
1/2 cup Thrive Sliced Onions
1 1/2 tbsp Thrive Espagnole Sauce
1 tsp Thrive Chef's Choice

To Make Jar: Layer ingredients in a quart jar. Seal tightly.

To Prepare: In a large saucepan bring 2 1/2 cups of water to a boil. Add contents of jar and let simmer 5-10 minutes.

Serve on a bun, in a lettuce wrap or eat plain as a stew. Enjoy!

Blackberry Mini Pies

Makes 6 Mini Pies

Pie Crust:
2 cups Flour (Thrive Gluten-Free Flour works)
1 tsp Salt
3/4 cup Shortening
1 tbsp Thrive Scrambled Egg Mix
3/4 cups Cold Water

Pie Filling:
3 cups Thrive Blackberries, refreshed
1/2 tbsp Lemon Juice
6 tbsp White Sugar
1 1/2 tbsp Corn Starch
Dash of Cinnamon

To Make Crust: Combine flour, egg powder, and salt. Cut in shortening until mixture is crumbly. Add water and stir until dough is formed. Put in refrigerator for an hour for easier rolling. Divide dough into 6 even pieces. Take 2/3 of each piece and form them in the bottom of a 6-muffin large muffin tray. Set in fridge while you prepare filling.

To Make Filling: Refresh blackberries. Drain and add lemon juice. Combine other ingredients in a separate bowl, then pour into blackberries. Mix thoroughly. Pour into cool pie shells. Top with remaining pie crust pieces (can do a woven pattern if desired. Sprinkle with sugar. Bake at 425 for about 30 minutes.

Broccoli & Cheese Rice in-a-Mug

Serves 1

1 Minute Rice Cup
1/2 cup Cold Water
2-3 Thrive Broccoli Florets, chopped smaller
3 tbsp Milk
1/2 tsp Cornstarch
4 tbsp Thrive Shredded Cheddar Cheese
Salt and Pepper, to taste

In mug, add water, chopped broccoli, milk, cornstarch, and cheese. Let refresh. Put Minute Rice cup in microwave for 1 minute.

Add cooked rice to mug. Microwave an additional 1:30 to 2 minutes. Stir and Enjoy!

Buffalo Ranch Chicken with Blue Cheese Flatbread

Serves 1

1 Thrive Chicken Salad To Go, prepared
1 Flat Bread
2 tbsp Ranch Dressing
2 tbsp Buffalo Sauce
Bacon Bits
1/2 cup Shredded Cheese
1/4 cup Blue Cheese
Parsley

Preheat oven to 350.

Prepare the To Go according to directions on package. Spread buffalo sauce and ranch on flat bread. Add refreshed To Go and crumble bacon bits over top. Cover with shredded cheese and blue cheese crumbles. Sprinkle with parsley.

Bake in oven for about 10 minutes or until cheese melts. Enjoy!

*If you do not have a To Go you can use 1/2 Cup Chopped Chicken, 1 tbsp Chopped Onions and 1 tbsp Celery!

Chicken & Green Mushroom Soup

By Rachel D.

Serves 1-2

1 can Cream of Mushroom Soup
1 can of Milk
1/2 cup Thrive Grilled Seasoned Chicken
1/4 cup Thrive Spinach
1/4 cup Thrive Asparagus
1/2 cup Thrive Instant Quinoa

Prepare soup with milk. Bring to a boil. Reduce heat and add remaining ingredients. Let simmer for 5 minutes.

Enjoy!

Chicken Fajita Scramble

Serves 1

1 Thrive Chicken Fajita To Go
4 tbsp Thrive Scrambled Egg Mix
9 tbsp Water

Crush up the To Go to make the pieces smaller. Mix scrambled egg mix and water in a microwave bowl. Add Fajita mix and let sit about 5 minutes to refresh.

Cook in microwave for 1 minute. If not done then cook at 30 second intervals until cooked.

Top with salsa and enjoy!

*Can be made on the stove as well.

Chicken Mushroom Gravy

Serves 1-2

2 tbsp Butter
1 tbsp Minced Garlic
1 cup Thrive Seasoned Chicken Slices
3/4 cup Thrive Mushrooms
1/2 cup Thrive Onion Slices
2 1/2 cups Water
1/2 to 3/4 tsp Thrive Chef's Choice
Salt and Pepper to taste
1/2 cup Thrive Velouté Sauce (Chicken Gravy)

In medium sized pan, melt butter and garlic together. Toss in chicken, mushrooms, and onions and toast slightly. Add water, Chef's Choice, and salt/pepper and simmer until refreshed. Add in Velouté, stir until mixed. Let simmer on low for a couple minutes until thick.

Serve over rice, noodles or Thrive Mashed Potatoes. Enjoy!

Chocolate Banana Mini Loaves

By Erin L.

Makes 4 Mini Loaves

1/2 cup Thrive Bananas, powdered
1/4 cup Water
3 Ripe Bananas
2/3 cup Sugar
1/3 cup Butter, melted
2 tbsp Thrive Scrambled Egg Mix
3 tbsp Water
1 tsp Vanilla
1 tsp Baking Soda
Pinch of Salt
1 1/2 cups Flour
1 cup Mini Chocolate Chips

Preheat oven to 350. Grease mini loaf pans.

Add water to powdered bananas. In a medium mixing bowl add peeled ripe bananas, sugar, and butter. Mix well. Add egg mix, water, and vanilla. Combine dry ingredients in a separate bowl and then gradually add to mixture. Once mixed add mini chips and pour into loaf pans.

Bake for 25-35 minutes or until cooked in the middle. Enjoy!

Cornbread Casserole

Serves 6

2 Eggs
1 box Jiffy Cornbread Mix
1/4 cup Butter, melted
1 cup Thrive Life Sour Cream, prepared*
2 cups Thrive Sweet Corn, refreshed
1 can Creamed Corn

*To Prepare Sour Cream: Combine 1 cup sour cream powder with 1/2 cup water. Whisk until smooth. Set aside.

Preheat oven to 350 degrees. Grease a 9x9 (or similar sized) baking dish. Refresh 2 cups of corn with 3/4 cups of water. Drain any excess water once refreshed.

In a medium bowl, whisk eggs lightly. Add in melted butter, prepared sour cream, refreshed Thrive corn and can of creamed corn. Mix together. Add in cornbread mix and stir until completely combined. Pour into dish and bake 45 minutes to 1 hour uncovered.

*When done, top will be golden and edges will be slightly cracked. Center will be firm. Enjoy!

Creamy Nutra-Packed Oats

by Rachel D.

Serves 2

1 cup Oats
3 tbsp Thrive Instant Quinoa
1 tsp Chia Seeds
5-6 Thrive Banana Slices, powdered
2 cups Water
Thrive Fruit Topping of Choice

Powder banana pieces and add all ingredients except fruit topping in a pot. Simmer for 10 minutes and stir a few times.

Take off heat, serve in bowl and top with Thrive fruit of choice- powdered, coarsely ground or whole (cherry pictured).

Crock Pot Chicken Pot Pie

Serves 4-6

2 cups Thrive Seasoned Chicken
1/2 cup Thrive Sliced Onions
1/2 cup Thrive Green Peas
1/2 cup Thrive Carrots
1/2 cup Thrive Corn
1/2 cup Thrive Green Beans
1 cup Thrive Potato Dices
1/2 cup Thrive Celery
Salt and Pepper to taste
1 tsp Garlic Powder
1/4 tsp Poultry Seasoning
1 can Cream of Chicken Soup
1 1/2 cups Milk
1 1/2 cups Water

Place all dry ingredients in the crock pot. Add liquid and mix.
Cook on low all day.
Serve with buttermilk biscuits!

*Add extra milk or water if too thick.

Easy Beef & Broccoli

by Christina R.

Serves 1

1/2 cup Thrive Shredded Beef
1/2 cup Thrive Broccoli
1/2 cup Thrive Egg Noodles
2 tbsp Thrive Espagnole Sauce (Beef Gravy)
Thrive Chef's Choice Seasoning to taste
1 1/2 cups Water

In microwave safe container combine first five ingredients.

Add water, stir and microwave for 6 minutes.

*Meal-in-a-jar option: Combine all ingredients except water into a pint sized jar. To cook, add 1 1/2 cups BOILING water. Let sit 10 minutes with lid on or until noodles are cooked.

Easy Taco Pasta

Serves 4

4 cups Noodles
1 1/2 cups Thrive Ground Beef
1 cup Thrive Tomato Dices
1/4 cup Thrive Chopped Onion
1/8-1/4 cup Thrive Green Chilies
6-8 cups Water

1 cup Salsa
1-2 tsp Taco Seasoning
Cheese

Bring 6-8 cups of water to a boil. Add noodles, beef, tomatoes, onions and chilies. Cook until noodles are soft. Drain out water.

Stir in salsa and taco seasoning. Sprinkle with cheese.

Food Truck Pulled Pork Over Mac & Cheese

Serves 1

1/2 cup Thrive Pulled Pork, refreshed
Salt and Pepper, to taste
1 cup Bob Evans Mac & Cheese (or your favorite brand)
Italian Bread Crumbs
BBQ Sauce
Thrive Green Onions

Refresh pulled pork with approximately 1/4 cup of hot water. Add salt pepper to season. Heat up mac and cheese.

On a plate, layer the mac & cheese, then the refreshed pulled pork. Sprinkle Italian breadcrumbs over top, drizzle with BBQ sauce and sprinkle with green onions! Enjoy!

*Delicious over homemade mac & cheese as well!

*Can substitute the pulled pork with Thrive Shredded Beef.

*Instead of bread crumbs use crunched up croutons.

Frozen Breakfast Pops

by Christina R.

Makes 4 Pops

2 cups Thrive Blueberry Yogurt Bites, refreshed
½ cup Thrive Very Berry Parfait Snackie

Refresh yogurt bites with about 4 TBS of water. Let sit for about 10 minutes until creamy (add more water little by little if not completely refreshed).

Stir in Very Berry Parfait mix. Freeze overnight in popsicle mold.

Enjoy!

Hamburger Helper Meal-in-a-Jar

Serves 2

1 1/2 cups Elbow Macaroni
1 cup Thrive Ground Beef
1 tsp Corn Starch
2 tsp Paprika
1 tsp Thrive Chopped Onions
1 tsp Garlic Powder
1 tsp Salt
1 tsp Sugar

1 cup Water
2 cups Milk
1 cup Thrive Cheddar Cheese

To Make Jar: Layer first 8 ingredients in your jar. Seal and label.

To Prepare: Add milk and water to medium size sauce pan. Dump in contents of jar and mix thoroughly. Bring to a boil, continuing to stir. Lower heat to simmer and cover until macaroni is cooked. Once cooked stir in cheese until melted and serve. Enjoy!

Hawaiian Pizza

by Christina R.

Serves 1

1 Thrive Island Style Pork To-Go
1 Thin Crust Pizza
1/2 cup BBQ Sauce
1 cup Mozzarella Cheese

Preheat oven to 425 degrees.
Follow instructions on To-Go pouch to refresh it and let sit for 15-20 minutes.

Put crust on pizza pan. Add BBQ sauce on top of pizza. Add refreshed To Go onto pizza (break with fingers a little bit and add before cheese to keep moisture in the pork)
Add cheese on pizza.

Bake until cheese is melted (approx. 10 minutes).

Home-Flavored Yogurt

by Rachel D.

Serves 1

1/2 cup Plain Yogurt
5-6 Pieces of Thrive Fruit (peach and cherry here)
Touch of Maple Syrup (optional)

Grind the fruit manually so you have a combination of small chunks and powder.

Mix fruit with plain yogurt and add a touch of maple syrup to desired sweetness!

Make ahead to have soft bits of fruit or eat right away to have a unique crunch!

Loaded Potato Soup in-a-Mug

Serves 1

2/3 cup Water
1 tsp Thrive Chicken Bouillon
1 cup Thrive Mashed Potatoes
2/3 cup Milk
1/4 tsp Garlic Powder
Salt and Pepper, to taste

Microwave water and bouillon in mug on high for 2 minutes. Whisk mashed potatoes, garlic powder and milk into chicken broth with a fork. Season with salt and pepper to taste. Microwave for about 45 seconds or until hot. Top with your favorite toppings.

Topping suggestions: sour cream, bacon, Thrive green onions.

Enjoy!

Mexican Breakfast Bowl

by Erin L.

Serves 1

1/2 cup Thrive Kale, refreshed
2 tbsp Thrive Scrambled Egg Mix
3 tbsp Water
1/2 cup Black Beans, cooked
1/4 cup Salsa
1/4 Avocado
1 tbsp Sweet & Spicy BBQ Sauce

Refresh kale in about 2 TBS of water. Heat up in a skillet. Combine scrambled egg mix with water. Add prepared scrambled egg mix to skillet with kale in it and cook.

Place cooked beans, eggs and kale in the bottom of the bowl. Top with avocado slices and salsa. Drizzle BBQ sauce over top.

Mrs. McG's Breakfast Sandwiches

by Shannon M.

Makes 2 Sandwiches

4 tbsp Thrive Scrambled Egg Mix
6 tbsp Water
1 cup Omelet Mixture (your choice of omelet fixings, refreshed)
Examples: chicken slices broken up into dice sized pieces, spinach, chopped onion and mixed bell peppers.
4 tbsp Tex Mex Cheese
4 tbsp Salsa
2 English Muffins, toasted

Refresh Omelet fixings and set aside. Combine eggs and water, then pour into a microwave omelet cooker. Layer with the refreshed omelet mixture.

Toast the English Muffins and top with salsa and cheese. Add half the omelet to each muffin.

*Can be made in frying pan as well.
*Can also be made with grocery store eggs.

Mrs. McG's Fruity Macaroons

by Shannon M.

Makes approx 15 cookies

2 cups Thrive Macaroon Cookie Mix
1/2 cup Hot Water
3 tbsp Thrive Strawberry Slices, powdered
3 tbsp Thrive Blueberries, powdered
3 tbsp Thrive Pineapple, powdered

Preheat oven to 350 degrees. Combine macaroon mix with hot water. Divide the prepared macaroon mix into 3 equal parts.

Stir in powdered fruit into each 1/3 of the mix. You may need a teaspoon of extra water. Scoop onto cookie sheet covered in parchment paper.

Bake for approximately 15 to 20 minutes.

*Use all of your favorite fruits!
*Dip the bottoms in melted chocolate!

Mrs. McG's Stuffed Peppers

by Shannon M.

Serves 9

9 Green Bell Peppers, hollowed out
6 cups Thrive Ground Beef, refreshed
1 cup Thrive Mushrooms, refreshed
1/2 cup Thrive Chopped Onion, refreshed
1 cup Thrive Instant Brown Rice, cooked
1 can Tomato Soup plus half can of water
Salt and Pepper or your favorite seasoning to taste

Preheat oven to 350 degrees.

Mix and refresh Thrive ingredients in about 3 cups of water. Once refreshed, drain excess water. Add seasonings of your choice along with the tomato soup/water mixture. Stuff the peppers.

Save either a small amount of tomato soup to put in the bottom of your baking dish or use water. Bake for 1-2 hours dependent on size and thickness of peppers.

*Recipe can be cut down to make only a few peppers at a time.
*Try using Thrive's Tomato Powder to make your own tomato soup to use.

Peach Coffee Cake

Makes 1 pie

Filling:
1/2 cup Butter, softened
1/2 cup Sugar
1/2 cup Peach Jam
4 tbsp Thrive Egg Mix
6 tbsp Water
2/3 cup Heavy Cream
2 cups Flour
2 1/2 tsp Baking Powder
1/2 tsp Baking Soda
1/2 tsp Salt
1 cup Thrive Peaches, refreshed

Topping:
2/3 cup Flour
1/4 cup Butter, melted
1/4 cup Peach Jam
1/2 cup Brown Sugar
1 tsp Cinnamon

Preheat oven to 375 degrees. Grease 13x9 baking pan. With mixer, cream butter and sugar. Add in peach jam and mix until well combined. Beat in eggs and water. Add in heavy cream while mixing on high to thicken the batter up. Beat for 5 minutes.

In mixing bowl, combine flour, baking powder, baking soda and salt. Add dry mixture to the wet and mix by hand until combined.

Spread into pan and place refreshed peaches on top of the batter. Combine topping ingredients and sprinkle clumps of topping evenly on peaches. Bake for 40 minutes. Enjoy!

*Make your own Peach Jam by using our Apricot Jam recipe but substitute Thrive Peaches.

Peanut Butter Energy Balls

Makes approx. 30 balls

1 cup Thrive Peanut Flour
2 tbsp Thrive Honey Crystals
1/2 tsp Salt
1/4 cup Coconut Oil
1/4 cup Cocoa
3 tbsp Chia Seeds
3 tbsp Thrive Instant Quinoa
1 cup Thrive Cherries, refreshed
3 tbsp Thrive Quick Oats
2/3 cup Water
Thrive Macaroon Mix

Mix all ingredients together except macaroon mix. Roll into balls, then roll in macaroon mix. Chill to make firm.

*I soaked my cherries over night in extra water (in refrigerator), then used the liquid as the water in my recipe.

Pesto-Mato-Tato Chicken

by Rachel D.

Serves 1

1/2 cup Thrive Grilled Chicken
1/4 cup Thrive Spinach
2 tbsp Tomato Powder
2 tbsp Pesto
2 tbsp Maple Syrup
1 cup Water

Mix all ingredients together in a pan and heat until chicken is refreshed and warmed through. Adjust liquid amount for desired consistency.

Eat by itself or serve over potatoes, rice, or noodles. Enjoy!

Rice & Black Bean Bake Dinner

by Kelly H.

Serves 4

2 cups Thrive Shredded Cheddar Cheese, refreshed
1 cup Black Beans, cooked
1 1/2 cups Thrive Diced Tomatoes, refreshed
1/4 cup Thrive Tomato Sauce, prepared
1 cup Rice, cooked
1 cup Thrive Sour Cream Powder, prepared

Preheat oven to 350 degrees.

Refresh cheese with 1/2 cup of COLD water, put in fridge for an hour. Cook rice and beans (both will expand to about 2 cups cooked). Prepare sour cream powder according to directions on can. Refresh diced tomatoes in about 2/3 cup of water.

In mixing bowl mix tomato sauce with 1 cup of water, mix well. Add in beans, tomatoes and rice. Stir. Stir in sour cream and 1 cup of the refreshed cheese. Mix together.

Pour into 9x13 baking pan, top with remaining cheese and bake for 20 minutes.

Serve with tortilla chips and enjoy!

*Add Thrive Green Chilies for a little kick!
*Make it saucier with 8 oz of salsa mixed in!

Sausage Quinoa Stir Fry

by Patti R.

Serves 1

1/4 cup Thrive Sausage Crumbles
2 tbsp Thrive Instant Quinoa
2 tbsp Thrive Chicken, powdered
2 tbsp Thrive Celery
1 tsp Thrive Chopped Onions
Thrive Broccoli
1/2 cup Hot Water
Soy Sauce

In a 1 cup glass measuring cup add the first 5 ingredients. Fill in the remaining room with broccoli. Refresh with hot water and let sit for about 5 minutes. Drain off any excess liquid.

In hot medium skillet, spritz with favorite oil. Stir fry mixture for 5-10 minutes. Add soy sauce to taste.

*Add to 1 cup coleslaw mix for some crunch!
*Use as a filling for lettuce wraps!
*Top with Thrive Green Onions!

Sausage Pineapple Casserole

by Laurie K.

Serves 12-16

1/2 cup Butter, softened
2 cups Sugar
8 Eggs
2 1/2 cups Thrive Sausage Crumbles
2 20-oz cans Crushed Pineapple, NOT drained
4 tbsp Lemon Juice
8 Slices Day-Old Bread, cubed (white or wheat)

In a mixing bowl, cream butter and sugar. Add the eggs, one at a time, beating well after each addition. Stir in sausage, pineapple and lemon juice. Fold in the bread cubes.

Pour into a greased 13x9x2 baking dish. Bake, uncovered, at 325° for 40-45 minutes or until set.

Scalloped Potatoes Meal-in-a-Jar

Serves 4

3 cups Dehydrated Potato Slices*
1/4 cup Thrive Instant Milk
1/4 cup Thrive Onion Slices
2 tbsp Flour
2 tbsp Corn Starch
1/2 tsp Salt
1/2 tsp Mustard Powder
1/8 tsp Pepper
1 tbsp Dried Chives (Optional)

2 3/4 cups Water
2 tbsp Butter

To Make Jar: Layer first 9 ingredients in jar. Add oxygen absorber and seal tight.

To Prepare: Dump contents of jar in baking dish. Add water and butter. Bake at 350 degrees until potatoes are tender.

Variations:
Add seasoned pork chops or ham steaks right on top of potatoes and bake until meat is cooked!!
Add cheese to make cheesy scalloped potatoes!

*Dehydrated potato slices can be found on Amazon

Strawberry Oatmeal Bars

Makes a 9x13 Pan

Crust:
3/4 cup Butter, melted
2/3 cup Brown Sugar
1 Egg
1 tsp Vanilla
1 cup Flour
2 cups Quick Oats
1/4 tsp Salt
1 tsp Baking Soda

Filling:
4 cups Thrive Strawberry Slices, refreshed
2 tbsp Flour

Topping:
1 cup Quick Oats
1/2 cup Flour
1/3 cup Sugar
1 tsp Baking Powder
1/3 cup Butter, melted

Preheat oven to 350. Line 9x13 pan with parchment paper.

For filling, add strawberries to a bowl with 1 cup water. Stir well and set aside to refresh. Drain any excess water once refreshed.

To make the crust mix butter and brown sugar in mixer, add egg and vanilla. Mix for 1 minute. Mix in dry ingredients until just combined. Press crust into pan evenly. Layer refreshed strawberries over crust and then sprinkle with the 2 tbsp flour.

To make the topping, add dry ingredients to bowl and add melted butter. Mix with a fork until crumbly. Sprinkle evenly over fruit. Bake for 25-30 minutes.

Street Corn Salad

Serves 4

3 cups Thrive Sweet Corn, refreshed
1/4 cup Thrive Cheddar Cheese, refreshed*
2 tbsp Mayo
2 tbsp Sour Cream
2 tbsp Thrive Cilantro
1 tbsp Lime Juice
1 tsp Chili Powder
1 tsp Garlic Powder
Salt and Pepper, to taste.

Refresh corn with 1 cup of warm water in a medium bowl. Add remaining ingredients to bowl. Cover and refrigerate for at least an hour. Enjoy!

*To refresh Thrive Cheddar Cheese. Combine 1/4 Cup Cheddar Cheese and 1 TBS cold water. Drizzle water over dry cheese and stir until well combined. Let sit about 35 minutes or until cheese is soft, stirring frequently. Keep in fridge.

**Add some bacon on top!

Vegetable Beef Soup

by Ellie T.

Serves 2

1/4 cup Thrive Ground Beef
1/4 tsp Thrive Onion Slices
3 tsp Thrive Beef Bouillon
1 tbsp Thrive Green Beans
1 tbsp Thrive Green Peas
1 tbsp Thrive Potato Dices
1 tbsp Thrive Carrots
1 tbsp Thrive Sweet Corn
1 tbsp Barley
1 tsp Thrive Tomato Powder
Salt and Pepper, to taste
3 cups Water

In small sauce pan add water and all ingredients. Cook until vegetables and barley are tender (about 8-10 minutes).

Enjoy!

Zucchini Corn Medley

by Kelly H.

Serves 4-5

1 1/2 cups Thrive Ground Beef
1 1/4 cups Thrive Sweet Corn
1 cup Thrive Zucchini
1 cup Thrive Diced Tomatoes
1/2 cup Thrive Chopped Onion
1/4 cup Thrive Green Chilies
2 tbsp Thrive Italian Seasoning
2 1/2 cups Hot Water

Mix all ingredients together and add hot water, let sit until refreshed.

"I'm so thankful for The Pantry Pack Club showing me creative ways to use my Thrive foods. Instead of just using it as snacks or as simple additions into stuff now I can make full Thrive meals, desserts, soups, etc. So quick & easy peasy too. Plus who doesn't love being a member of a cool club 😎?"

~Angela Turgeon,
Pantry Pack Club Member

Blast from the Past Pack

Cherry Peach Smoothie
Chicken Stew with Butternut Squash
Faux Pumpkin Pie
Gourmet Mashed Potatoes
Peach Crumble Muffins
Pears and Cherry Crisp
Pepper Chicken Stir Fry
Sausage & Pepper Skillet
Simple Cherry Sauce
Zuppa Toscana Soup Meal-in-a-Jar

Cherry Peach Smoothie

Serves 1

1/2 cup Thrive Peaches
1/2 cup Thrive Sweet Cherries
2 cups Water

Refresh fruit in water for 10-15 minutes. Blend and enjoy.

*Add ice to make it an icy smoothie
*Add in some vanilla yogurt and blend
*Top with whipped cream
*Pour into popsicle molds and freeze

Chicken Stew with Butternut Squash

Serves 4-5

2 tbsp Oil
1 tsp Minced Garlic
1 tbsp Thrive Chopped Onions
1/2 cup Thrive Carrots
1 cup (heaping) Thrive Butternut Squash
1 cup Thrive Diced Potatoes
1 cup Thrive Grilled Chicken Slices
1 tsp Thrive Chicken Bouillon
1 tsp Dried Parsley
Salt and Pepper, to taste
1 tbsp Thrive Tomato Sauce
8 cups Water

In a skillet, heat oil and sauté garlic and onions. Add water and all ingredients except tomato sauce, bring to a boil. Reduce to a simmer for 15 minutes, stir in tomato sauce and enjoy!

Faux Pumpkin Pie

Makes 1 Pie

1 Pre-Made Pie Shell
1 1/2 cups Thrive Butternut Squash
1/3 cup Brown Sugar
1 tbsp Pumpkin Pie Spice
6 tbsp Thrive Scrambled Egg Mix
2 tbsp Flour
2 tbsp Butter (or Thrive butter powder)

Bake pre-made pie shell as per directions.

In a medium saucepan, refresh the squash with the spices and sugar in two cups water. Simmer for 15 minutes. Mash the mixture and add egg mix, flour, and butter. Mix well. Pour into baked pie shell.

Bake at 350 degrees for 50 minutes or until toothpick comes out clean.

Let cool and slice. Serve and enjoy with whipped cream or ice cream!

Gourmet Mashed Potatoes

Serves 2

1 cup Thrive Mashed Potatoes
3 tbsp Thrive Green Onions
1/2 tsp Thrive Chicken Bouillon
1 tbsp Thrive Butter Powder
1 tbsp Thrive Sour Cream Powder
1 1/2 cups Boiling Water

Combine all ingredients in a small saucepan, add boiling water, stir. Add more water if you prefer thinner mashed potatoes. Enjoy!

*Sprinkle with cheese!
*Add Garlic for garlic mashed!
*Add bacon!

Peach Crumble Muffins

Makes 8 Lrg. or 12 Sm. Muffins

Muffins:
1 1/4 cups Flour
1 1/2 tsp Baking Powder
1/2 tsp Salt
2/3 cup Sugar
2 cups Thrive Peaches, refreshed
1/2 cup Milk
1 Egg
1/4 cup Vegetable Oil

Topping:
1/4 cup Flour
1/4 cup Sugar
1 pinch Cinnamon
3 tbsp Unsalted Butter (cold)

Preheat oven for 350 degrees. Prepare a large muffin tin with 8 muffin cups (or 12 regular).

In a bowl, crunch up peaches then add about 2 cups of water to refresh. Stir and set aside to refresh for 10-15 minutes. Drain any excess liquid once refreshed.

In medium bowl add flour, baking powder, salt and sugar. Combine. Add all but 3/4 cup of peaches (reserve for topping) mix thoroughly. Add in milk, egg, oil and stir together until mixed. Portion batter out into muffin tins.

Combine flour, sugar, and cinnamon in small bowl, stir. Add cold butter in chunks and break up into the flour mixture and mix until it resembles coarse crumbs.

Top muffins with remaining chunks of peaches and a spoonful of the topping. Bake for about 20-30 minutes until golden brown.

Pears and Cherry Crisp

Serves 9

Filling:
1 cup Thrive Sweet Cherries
2 cups Thrive Pears
1/2 cup Brown Sugar
1 tbsp Flour

Topping:
1 cup Oats
1/2 cup Brown Sugar
1/2 cup Flour
1/2 cup Pecans, finely chopped
1/2 cup Butter (or Coconut Oil), melted

Preheat oven to 350 degrees. Pour cherries and pears into a square baking dish. Pour 1 cup of water over top and stir around. Allow to refresh while preparing the topping.

Mix all topping ingredients together and set aside.

Add brown sugar and flour to fruit mixture and stir until combined.

Sprinkle topping over top of the fruit and bake for 30-40 minutes or until topping is golden brown.

Pepper Chicken Stir Fry

Serves 3-4

Marinade:
2 tbsp Soy Sauce
1 clove Garlic, minced
1 tbsp Toasted Sesame Oil
1/2 tsp Ground Black Pepper

Sauce:
3 tbsp Soy Sauce
1/2 tsp Worcestershire Sauce
1 tbsp White Vinegar
1/2 tsp Ground Black Pepper
1 tbsp Corn Starch
1/4 cup Water

1 cup Thrive Grilled Chicken
1 tbsp Corn Starch (to toss)

1 cup Thrive Green Peppers
1 cup Thrive Red Bell Peppers
1/2 cup Thrive Sliced Onions
2 cloves Garlic, minced
1/4 tsp Ground Ginger

2 tbsp Vegetable Oil (to stir fry)

Refresh chicken in 1/3 cup of water. Combine marinade ingredients in medium bowl and add refreshed chicken. Let stand for 10-15 minutes. Meanwhile, refresh peppers and onions in 3/4 cups of water. Combine sauce ingredients and set aside.

Drain chicken and toss with cornstarch. Add vegetable oil to frying pan and heat up. Cook chicken for 3-4 minutes, stirring to get both sides cooked. Drain peppers and onions and add to frying pan. Stir for 1-2 minutes until heated through. Add garlic and ginger, cook for one minute. Stir in sauce and cook until heated and thickened.

Serve over rice or with additional steamed vegetables on the side.

Sausage & Pepper Skillet

Serves 2

2 tbsp Oil
1 tsp Garlic
1 tbsp Thrive Chopped Onions
1/2 cup Thrive Sausage Crumbles
1/3 cup Thrive Red Bell Pepper
1/3 cup Thrive Green Peppers
2 1/2 cups Water
1 tsp Thrive Chicken Bouillon
1 cup Thrive Instant Rice
1 tbsp Parsley
Salt and Pepper, to taste

In medium skillet sauté onions and garlic in oil. Toss in peppers and sausage, cook for 1 minute. Add water and bouillon to pan and bring to boil. Add in rice and parsley. Cover and cook for 10 minutes until rice is tender. Add salt and pepper to taste.

Simple Cherry Sauce

Makes 1-2 Servings

1/2 cup Thrive Sweet Cherries
1 cup Water
1/2 cup Sugar
1 tsp Lemon Juice
1 tbsp Corn Starch

Bring water and cherries to boil. Reduce to simmer for 15 minutes. Add more water if it boils down too much.

Mash cherries with spoon until desired consistency. Stir in lemon juice and corn starch.

Serve on cake, ice cream, brownies, yogurt or even oatmeal! Enjoy!

Zuppa Toscana Soup Meal-in-a-Jar

Serves 4-6

1/4 cup Thrive Sour Cream Powder
3 tbsp Thrive Velouté Gravy
1 tbsp Thrive Chicken Bouillon
3 tbsp Thrive Chopped Onions
1/2 tsp Garlic Powder
1/2 tsp Thrive Chef's Choice Seasoning
3/4 cup Thrive Spinach
3/4 cup Thrive Diced Potatoes
3/4 cup Thrive Sausage Crumbles
3/4 cup Thrive Mashed Potatoes

To Make Jar: Add ingredients to jar in order listed for a prettier jar, add ingredients in reverse order if you want to do heaping servings.

To Prepare: Pour 5 cups of water into a large saucepan. Add contents of jar and stir thoroughly. Cook 10-12 minutes or until potatoes are soft.

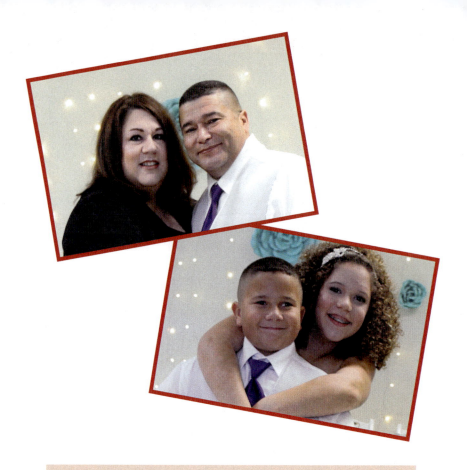

"Thrive life has been a game changer for me!! I'm a self proclaimed "Lazy Cook" because before Thrive Life my family pretty much lived on pre-fab food that was easy to toss in the oven. Using Thrive is way easier, we end up having meals that I would never have made before and it has turned me into a GOOD cook!! Not going to lie, I'm still a lazy cook but that's ok, Thrive Life makes it ok!"

~Christina Riostirado,
Meals in Minutes Co-Author

Cinco de Mayo Pack

Chicken or Beef Enchiladas
Chicken Santa Fe Dip-in-a-Jar
Chili
Refried Bean Dip
Refried Bean Soup
Spanish Rice
Taco Soup

Chicken or Beef Enchiladas

Serves 3

1 cup Thrive Grilled Chicken (or Thrive Ground Beef)
1 can Refried Beans
1/4 cup Thrive Tomato Powder
1 tsp Taco Seasoning
1 tsp Thrive Green Chili Peppers
1 cup Water
6 6-Inch Tortillas
1 cup Thrive Cheddar Cheese, refreshed

Preheat oven to 350 degrees. In a small bowl refresh chicken or beef with warm water according to directions on can. Once refreshed, drain off excess water and mix in refried beans.
In separate bowl mix water, tomato powder, taco seasoning, chili peppers.

Cover bottom of baking dish with sauce mixture. Scoop meat and bean mixture into tortillas and roll. Place in row in baking dish. Cover with remaining sauce and refreshed cheese (according to directions on can)

Bake for 30 minutes. Enjoy!

Chicken Santa Fe Dip-in-a-Jar

Serves 4

1 cup Thrive Tomato Dices
1/4 cup Thrive Green Chili Peppers
1 cup Thrive Grilled Chicken, crushed
1 cup Thrive Shredded Cheddar Cheese
2 tbsp Buffalo Sauce
8 oz Cream Cheese

To Make Jar: Layer first four ingredients into the jar. Make a tag with directions.

To Prepare: Refresh all Thrive ingredients in 2 cups of water. Drain off excess water and mix in cream cheese and buffalo sauce. Heat until melted and creamy.

*Serve with tortillas or over pasta for a full meal.

Chili

Serves 2

1/2 cup Thrive Ground Beef
1/2 cup Thrive Refried Beans
1/2 cup Thrive Tomato Dices
1/4 cup Thrive Sweet Corn
1/4 cup Thrive Tomato Powder
2 tbsp Thrive Green Chili Peppers
2 tsp Chili Powder
1 tsp Minced Garlic
1 tsp Chili Flakes
3 cups Water

In medium sauce pan add all ingredients and bring to boil. Reduce to simmer for ten minutes.
Let rest for five minutes and serve!

Refried Bean Dip

Serves 4

1 can Refried Beans
1 pkg Taco Seasoning
1/4 cup Thrive Green Chili Peppers, refreshed
1/2 cup Sour Cream
1 cup Thrive Tomato Dices, refreshed
1 tsp Thrive Chopped Onions, refreshed
1 cup Thrive Shredded Cheese, refreshed

Combine refried beans, taco seasoning, and chili peppers for the first layer. Second layer is just sour cream. Third layer is refreshed onions and tomatoes. Final layer, top with shredded cheese.

Serve with Tortilla Chips.

Refried Bean Soup

Serves 4

1 cup Thrive Tomato Dices
1/4 cup Thrive Tomato Sauce
1/2 tsp Minced Garlic
1 cup Thrive Refried Beans
2 tsp Thrive Chicken Bouillon
1 tsp Cilantro
5 cups Water

Bring all ingredients to a boil. Reduce heat and simmer for ten minutes.

Serve with corn chips or tortillas and sour cream.

Spanish Rice

Serves 2

1/2 cup Thrive Grilled Chicken
2 tbsp Thrive Green Chili Peppers
1/4 cup Thrive Red Peppers (crushed)
1/4 cup Thrive Tomato Dices
2 tbsp Thrive Tomato Sauce
1 cup Instant Brown Rice
1 tsp Cilantro
3 cups Water

Add all ingredients into a large skillet and bring to a boil. Remove from heat, cover with lid, and let rest 10 minutes.

Taco Soup

Serves 2

1/2 cup Thrive Ground Beef
1/2 cup Thrive Sweet Corn
1/4 cup Thrive Green Chili Peppers
1/4 cup Thrive Red Peppers
1 tsp Thrive Chicken Bouillon
2 tsp Thrive Tomato Sauce
1 tsp Taco Seasoning
2 cups Water

In a medium sauce pan, bring all ingredients to boil then reduce to simmer for 10 minutes. Enjoy!

Bonus Recipes

Beef Stroganoff Meal-in-a-Jar
Black Bean Salsa
Buttermilk
Creamy Skillet Bacon Cheeseburger Dip
Crock Pot Lasagna
Lemon Juice
Lemon Peach Italian Soda
Mexican Spinach Dip
Messy Philly Cheesesteak Meal-in-a-Jar
Oat Flour Pancakes w/ Blackberry Syrup
Potato Beef Tacos

Beef Stroganoff Meal-in-a-Jar

Serves 2

3/4 cup Thrive Beef Slices
3/4 cup Thrive Mushroom Slices
1/4 cup Thrive Onion Slices
1 1/2 cups Egg Noodles
1/2 cup Thrive Sour Cream Powder
2 tsp Thrive Tomato Powder
1/4 cup Thrive Espagnole Sauce (Beef Gravy)
1 tsp Thrive Beef Bouillon
1 1/2 tsp Garlic Powder

To Make Jar: Layer ingredients in order listed in quart-sized mason jar.

To Prepare: Dump contents of jar into sauce pan with 4 cups of cold water. Let sit for 10 minutes. Bring to a boil, then turn down and simmer for 15 minutes, stirring occasionally. Add additional water if too thick. Serve and enjoy!

Black Bean Salsa (Texas Caviar)

Serves 8-10

1/2 tsp Salt
1/2 tsp Pepper
1/4 cup Olive Oil
3/4 cup Vinegar
1/3 cup Sugar

1 can each: Black Eyed Peas, Pinto Beans and Black Beans
1 cup Thrive Corn, refreshed
1/2 cup Thrive Green Bell Peppers, refreshed
1/2 cup Thrive Red Bell Peppers, refreshed
1 small jar Pimento or Roasted Red Peppers

Mix together first 5 ingredients in a small bowl and set aside. Rinse and drain the beans. Refresh corn and bell peppers in about 1 cup of water. Drain any remaining liquid. Combine beans, corn, peppers, and pimento in a large bowl. Pour liquid mixture over top and stir until well-coated.

Make 4-6 hours ahead of time. Serve with tortilla chips as an appetizer or side dish.

Buttermilk

Makes 1 Cup

1 cup Milk
1 tbsp Thrive Lemon Juice (see recipe on page 119)

Make lemon juice using the lemon juice recipe on page 119.

Mix mik and lemon juice. Refrigerate. Use cup for cup in recipes that call for buttermilk.

Creamy Skillet Bacon Cheeseburger Dip

Serves 6-8

1-2 tbsp Olive Oil
1/4 cup Thrive Chopped Onions
1 cup Thrive Ground Beef
1/2 cup Thrive Bacon TVP (or 7 Slices of Bacon)
1 1/2 cup Thrive Cheddar Cheese, divided
8 oz Cream Cheese, softened
1 tbsp Worcestershire Sauce
1 tsp Garlic Powder
Salt and Pepper, to taste
Dill Pickles and Parsley, as garnish (optional)

Preheat oven to 350 degrees. Spray an 8 inch cast iron skillet or 1.5-2 qt baking dish with cooking spray.

In medium bowl, refresh onions, ground beef, tvp, and 1 cup cheddar cheese with 3/4 cup of warm water. Drain out excess water once refreshed. Refresh remaining 1/2 cup of cheese in separate bowl with 3-4 TBS of water. Mix in remaining ingredients. Transfer into prepared skillet or baking dish. Sprinkle remaining refreshed cheese on top.

Bake 12-15 minutes until bubbly. Garnish and serve!! Enjoy!

Crock Pot Lasagna

Serves 8-10

1 cup Thrive Tomato Sauce
7 1/2 cups Water, divided
2 cups Thrive Ground Beef
1/4 cup Thrive Red Bell Peppers
1/4 cup Thrive Red Bell Peppers
1/2 cup Thrive Mushrooms
1/2 cup Thrive Spinach
1/2 cup Thrive Sliced Onions
2 cups Shredded Mozzarella Cheese
3 cups Cottage Cheese or Ricotta Cheese
1 box Uncooked Lasagna Noodles

In medium sauce pan, heat 4 cups of water and whisk in tomato sauce until combined. Remove from heat. In medium bowl, refresh ground beef, peppers, mushrooms, spinach, and onions in 3 1/2 cups of warm water, don't drain.

Spoon 1 cup sauce in bottom of 4-quart crock pot. Place 2 uncooked lasagna noodles on sauce in crock pot. Spread 1/3 meat/veggie/water mixture on top of noodles. Spread 3/4 cup cottage cheese over meat. Sprinkle 1/2 cup mozzarella cheese over cottage cheese. Add another layer of uncooked noodles.

Repeat until you have 3-4 layers. Sprinkle remaining mozzarella over top. Cook on low for 4 hours.

Lemon Juice

Makes 1/2 Cup

1/2 cup Water
2 tbsp Thrive Classic Lemonade

Never buy lemon juice again! Mix water and lemonade together and refrigerate.

This makes a tart lemon juice, add more water if you want it less tart.

Lemon Peach Italian Soda

Serves 4

Peach Syrup:
2 cups Thrive Peach Slices
1 cup Thrive Simply Peach Drink Mix
1/2 tbsp Thrive Classic Lemonade
1 cup Sugar
1/3 tbsp Vanilla
1 1/2 cups Water

Italian Soda:
1/4 cup Peach Syrup
1/2 cup Ice
1/2 cup Soda Water
1 tbsp Heavy Cream

To Make Syrup: Add peaches to blender or food processor and puree into powder. Add remaining syrup ingredients and mix well.

For Each Soda: Add 1/4 cup peach syrup, 1/2 cup ice, 1/2 cup soda water, and 1 tbsp cream. Stir well to incorporate.

Mexican Spinach Dip

Serves 8-10

8 oz Cream Cheese, softened
1/3 cup Sour Cream
2 tbsp Thrive Green Chili Peppers (add more to taste)
1 cup Thrive Tomato Dices
2 tbsp Thrive Chopped Onions
1 cup Thrive Chopped Spinach
3 cups Extra Sharp Cheese
1 tsp Salt
1/2 tsp Chili Powder
1/2 tsp Ground Cumin

Preheat oven to 350.

In a medium mixing bowl, blend the cream cheese and sour cream together. In a separate bowl, combine all Thrive ingredients and add about 3/4 cups of water to refresh. Drain off any excess water once refreshed. Add refreshed veggies to cream cheese mixture. Add in seasonings and cheese and mix thoroughly.

Spread mixture in an 8 inch square baking dish (spray with non-stick spray). Bake for 25-30 minutes until golden and bubbly. Serve with tortillas as an appetizer or side dish.

Messy Philly Cheesesteak Meal-in-a-Jar

Serves 1

1/2 cup Thrive Shredded Beef
3 tbsp Thrive Red Bell Peppers
3 tbsp Thrive Sliced Onions
3 tbsp Thrive Mushrooms
1/4 cup Thrive Mozzarella Cheese
1 tsp Thrive Espangol Sauce (or other Beef Gravy)
1/4 tsp Thrive Chef's Choice Seasoning
1 tsp Minced Garlic

To Make Jar: Put all ingredients into a 1/2 pint sized jar.

To Prepare: Add 1/2 to 3/4 cup of boiling water. Stir and cover. Let sit for 5-10 minutes until everything is refreshed. Eat right out of the jar or put on a bun!

Oat Flour Pancakes w/ Blackberry Syrup

Makes 12 Pancakes

Blackberry Syrup:
1 cup Thrive Blackberries, powdered
1 cup Water
1/4 cup Sugar

Bring ingredients to a boil in a small saucepan. Let simmer for 10 minutes. (Makes about 1 1/2 cups of syrup)

Pancakes:
3 cups Quick Oats, powdered (Makes 1 1/2 cups Oat Flour)
2 tbsp Sugar
2 tsp Baking Powder
1/2 tsp Salt
4 tbsp Butter, melted
1 cup Buttermilk
1 tsp Vanilla
1/2 cup Water

Preheat nonstick skillet over medium heat while you prepare batter.

In a large mixing bowl, whisk all dry ingredients together. In a second mixing bowl whisk together the wet ingredients. Add wet mix to the dry mix and whisk thoroughly. Batter should be pourable. If not, whisk in more water 1 tablespoon at a time.

Add 1/4 cup of batter to the hot skillet. Cook until air bubbles form and stay open. Flip and cook on other side until golden brown.

Potato Beef Tacos

Serves 6

2 16 oz Bags Frozen Tater Tots or Hash Browns
1 cup Thrive Ground Beef
1/2 Package Taco Seasoning
1 1/2 cups Shredded Mexican Cheese Blend
1 cup Salsa
Shredded Lettuce
Sour Cream and Guacamole (optional)

Refresh ground beef and taco seasoning with 1/2 cup of hot water for about 5-8 minutes.

Bake tater tots on a foil lined cookie sheet at 425 degrees for 15 minutes.

Sprinkle potatoes with beef mixture and cheese. Bake 3 to 5 minutes longer or just until cheese is melted. Top with remaining ingredients. Enjoy!

Strawberry Basil Lemonade

Makes 2 Quarts

2 tbsp Thrive Classic Lemonade
1 cup Sugar (or sweetener of choice)
2 qt Water
1 1/2 Cups Thrive Life Strawberry Slices
Thrive Life Basil
1-2 cups Ice

Make up lemonade with water and sugar. In the blender add strawberries, ice and a couple of shakes of basil. Add already mixed lemonade. Blend to make a slushy. Enjoy!

Equivalents & Substitutions

Grains	
1 cup wheat kernels	1 1/2 cups wheat flour
1 cup flour	~ 3/4 cup wheat kernels
1 cup popcorn kernels	1 1/2 cups cornmeal
1 cup cornmeal	~ 3/4 cup popcorn kernels
Legumes	
4 T. dried white beans	5 T. white bean flour
15 oz can of beans	1/2 cup dry beans 1 1/2 cups cooked beans
1 lb of dry beans	2 cups dry beans 6 cups cooked beans
Fruits	
1 apple	1 cup freeze-dried apples
1 banana	1 cup freeze-dried bananas
1 cup berries	1 cup freeze-dried berries
1 peach	1 cup freeze-dried peaches
1 cup pineapple	1 cup freeze-dried pineapple
Meats	
1 lb chicken or meat	1 1/2 cup FD chicken/meat 1 pt home-canned chicken/meat

	Cheese
1 cup cheese	1 cup freeze-dried cheese, must reconstitute first for melting
	Vegetables
1 small onion	1/4 cup dehydrated onion 1/2 cup freeze-dried onion
3 stalks celery	1/2 cup freeze-dried celery
1 bell pepper	1/2 cup dehydrated peppers 1 cup freeze-dried peppers
1 cup chopped vegetables	1/3 cup dehydrated veggies 1 cup freeze-dried vegetables
	Milk
1 cup milk	Mix 3 tbsp powdered milk + 1 cup water.
14 oz sweetened condensed milk	Mix 1/2 cup hot water, 1 cup powdered milk, 1 cup sugar, 1 tbsp butter. Blend very well.
12 oz can evaporated milk	Mix 1 1/2 cups water, 1/2 cup + 1 tbsp powdered milk. Blend.
1 cup buttermilk	Mix 1 tbsp lemon juice or white vinegar, 3 tbsp powdered milk, 1 cup water. Let sit 5 minutes.
	Other
1 egg	Mix 1 tbsp powdered eggs + 2 tbsp water.
1 cup sour cream	Mix 1 cup sour cream powder + 1 cup water.
1 cup butter	Mix 1 cup butter powder + 1 cup water.

Index (by Recipe Type)

Breakfast

Apple Cinnamon Muffins .... page 32
Blackberry Cornmeal Muffins .... page 11
Carrot pineapple muffins .... page 12
Chicken Fajitas Scramble .... age 63
Cornbread Applesauce Muffins .... page 44
Creamy Nutri Packed Oats .... page 67
Dutch Apple Baby .... page 45
Egg Boats page22
Frozen Breakfast Pops .... page 72
Home Flavoured Yogurt page75
Mexican Breakfast Bowl page77
Mrs McG's Breakfast Sandwich .... page 78
Oat Flour Pancakes with Blackberry Syrup .... page 123
Omelette-in-a-Bag page25
Peach Crumble Muffins .... page 98
Peanut Butter Energy Balls .... page 82
Strawberry Oatmeal Bars .... page 88

Drinks

Apple Pie Smoothie .... page 8
Cherry Peach Smoothie .... page 94
Lemon Peach Italian Soda .... page 120
Peanut Butter and Jelly Smoothie .... page 26
Red White and Blue Smoothie .... page 40
Strawberry Basil Lemonade .... page 125

Sides & Appetizers

Beans and Berries	page 20
Black Bean Salsa (Texas Caviar)	page 115
Buffalo Ranch Chicken with Blue Cheese Flatbread	page 61
Chicken Bacon Salad Wrap	page 36
Chicken Santa Fe Dip-in-a-Jar	page 107
Cornbread Casserole	page 66
Creamy Skillet Bacon Cheeseburger Dip	page 117
Curried Cauliflower	page 15
Gourmet Mashed Potatoes	page 97
Grilled Bean and Apple Salad	page 23
Homemade Cornbread	page 16
Loaded Cauliflower	page 17
Mexican Spinach Dip	page 121
Mozzarella Green Bean Salad	page 24
Refried Bean Dip	page 109
Sausage and Pepper Skillet	page 101
Scalloped Potatoes Meal-in-a-Jar	page 87
Spanish Rice	page 111
Street Corn Salad	page 89
Zucchini Corn Medley	page 91

Soups, Stews, Chili

Chicken and Green Mushroom Soup	page 92
Chicken and Bean Chili	page 13
Chicken Noodle Soup Meal-in-a-Jar	page 14
Chicken Stew with Butternut Squash	page 95
Chili	page 108
Loaded Potato Soup in-a-Mug	page 76
Refried Bean Soup	page 110
Taco Soup	page 112
Tomato Soup and Cheesy Dippers	page 29
Vegetable Beef Soup	page 90
Zuppa Toscana Soup Meal-in-a-Jar	page 103

Main Courses

Apricot Chicken	page 33
Beef Fajitas Meal-in-a-Jar	page 57
Beef Philly Cheesesteak Meal-in-a-Jar	page 58
Beef Stroganoff Meal-in-a-Jar	page 114
Broccoli and Cheese Rice in-a-Mug	page 60
Buffalo Chicken Wraps	page 35
Chicken / Beef Enchiladas	page 106
Chicken Parmigiana	page 37
Chicken Salad	page 38
Crock Pot Chicken Pot Pie	page 68
Crock Pot Lasagna	page 118
Easy Beef and Broccoli	page 69
Easy Taco Pasta	page 70
Food Truck Pulled Pork over Mac and Cheese	page 71
Ground Beef and Potato Casserole	page 46
Ground Beef Stroganoff	page 47
Hamburger Helper Meal-in-a-Jar	page 73
Hawaiian Pizza	page 74
Jamaican Beef Patties	page 48
Mrs McG's Stuffed Peppers	page 80
Pepper Chicken Stir Fry	page 100
Pesto Mato Tato Chicken	page 83
Potato Beef Tacos	page 124
Pulled Pork Goulash	page 49
Pulled Pork Sliders	page 50
Rice and Black Bean Bake Dinner	page 84
Sausage Pineapple Casserole	page 86
Sausage Quinoa Stir Fry	page 85
Sweet and Sour Pork	page 51
Taco In a Bag	page 52
Tomato Broccoli Casserole	page 28
Tourtiere	page 53

Meal-in-a-Jars

Beef Fajitas Meal-in-a-Jar .... page 57
Beef Philly Cheesesteak Meal-in-a-Jar .... page 58
Beef Stroganoff Meal-in-a-Jar .... page 114
Camping Quesadillas Meal-in-a-Jar .... page 21
Chicken Noodle Soup Meal-in-a-Jar .... page 13
Hamburger Helper Meal-in-a-Jar.. page 73
Messy Cheese Philly Cheesesteak Meal-in-a-Jar .... page 122
Pork Goulash Meal-in-a-Jar... page 49
Sausage Noodle Salad Meal-in-a-Jar .... page 27
Scalloped Potatoes Meal-in-a-Jar .... page 87
Zuppa Toscana Soup Meal-in-a-Jar .... page 103

Desserts

Apple Pear Cobbler.. page 56
Apple Pinto Bean Tart .... page 9
Apricot Jam / Topping / Compote... page 34
Blackberry Apple Crumble .... page 10
Blackberry Mini Pies .... page 59
Chocolate Banana Mini Loaves .... page 65
Faux Pumpkin Pie .... page 96
Mrs McG's Fruity Macaroons .... page 79
Peach Coffee Cake .... page 81
Pears and Cherry Crisp .... page 99
Patriotic Jello .... page 39
Rice Pudding.. page 41
Simple Cherry Sauce .... page 102

Other

Buttermilk .... page 116
Chicken Mushroom Gravy .... page 64
Lemon Juice page119

Meals in Minutes

Made in the USA
Las Vegas, NV
12 February 2025